MW00888503

Comprehending Functional Text

Instruction • Practice • Assessment

Authors: Schyrlet Cameron and Suzanne Myers
Editors: Mary Dieterich and Sarah M. Anderson
Proofreader: Margaret Brown

COPYRIGHT © 2013 Mark Twain Media, Inc.

ISBN 978-1-62223-000-6

Printing No. CD-404182

Mark Twain Media, Inc., Publishers
Distributed by Carson-Dellosa Publishing LLC

Visit us at www.carsondellosa.com

Table of Contents

To the Teacher

Students are surrounded by nonfiction text. They must have the ability to understand its purpose, gather key ideas and details, make inferences, and evaluate the information. One type of nonfiction is informational text. Three subgenres of informational text are exposition, argument, and functional text. Examples of functional text are brochures, food nutrition labels, menus, and class schedules.

The purpose of functional text is to help the reader accomplish real-world tasks. This requires skills such as following multi-step, written directions; recognizing patterns and structures; and locating and interpreting information contained in functional text documents. These reading skills are critical in preparing students for college and career readiness: a goal of the Common Core State English Language Arts Standards.

Comprehending Functional Text: Instruction, Practice, and Assessment is designed to offer teachers a wide variety of instructional options to meet the diverse learning styles of middle-school students. The format of this book is divided into five sections.

- **Instructional Resources** introduce the types, features, and structures of functional text. These handouts can be used as teacher-directed introductory lessons.

- **Practice Activities** provide students with opportunities to work with functional text documents. Each lesson features a document followed by skill-building questions and an activity.

- The **Learning Stations** engage students in small-group activities. Students are able to examine, analyze, and discuss a functional text document.

- **Assessment Prep** tests students' understanding of functional text documents. This section features a document followed by comprehension questions written in standardized test format.

- **Bulletin Board Ideas and More** are activities that can be used to reinforce and extend student learning.

This book can be used for independent practice, small-group or classroom instruction, and as homework. The activities are designed to supplement or enhance the regular classroom reading curriculum or can be used with ESL and Title I students.

Common Core State Standards Matrix

English Language Arts Standards: Reading Informational Text

Assignment	RI.6.1	RI.6.2	RI.6.3	RI.6.4	RI.6.5	RI.6.6	RI.6.7	RI.6.8	RI.6.9	RI.6.10	RI.7.1	RI.7.2	RI.7.3	RI.7.4	RI.7.5	RI.7.6	RI.7.7	RI.7.8	RI.7.9	RI.7.10	RI.8.1	RI.8.2	RI.8.3	RI.8.4	RI.8.5	RI.8.6	RI.8.7	RI.8.8	RI.8.9	RI.8.10
Classified Advertisements	X			X			X		X		X			X			X		X		X			X			X		X	
Email	X			X		X					X			X		X					X			X		X				
Family Calendar	X										X										X									
Food Nutrition Label	X			X			X				X			X			X				X			X			X			
Internet Search Screen	X			X			X		X		X			X			X		X		X			X			X			
Recipe	X			X							X			X							X			X						
Restaurant Menu	X								X		X								X		X								X	
Safety Rules	X			X							X			X							X			X						
Sales Flyer	X										X										X									
Text Message	X										X										X									
Learning Stations Activity	X			X			X	X			X			X				X			X			X				X		
Text Mapping					X										X										X					
Text Feature Wall					X		X								X										X					
Functional Text					X							X			X							X			X					
Collection Notebook		X																												

Grade Level

What Is Functional Text?

Functional text is everywhere. Did you go to a ballgame last night? Were you handed a roster of players? The roster is an example of functional text. After the game, did you go to a restaurant? If so, you probably ordered off a menu. The menu is another example of functional text.

The purpose of **functional text** is to give you specific information or to help you perform a day-to-day task. Some examples of functional text are brochures, food nutrition labels, menus, recipes, and class schedules.

There are two ways to read functional text. One way is to **skim the text** to find the needed information. Another way is to **read word for word**. While reading, you should be thinking about what is being read and deciding if the information is useful.

When reading functional text, you should look at how the information is presented. For example, is the information arranged in chronological order or step by step? Has the author used text features such as illustrations or bold words to emphasize key points? Paying attention to these details will help you to locate information and understand what you are reading.

Examples of Functional Text

• Advertisements	• Instructions	• Recipes
• Announcements	• Internet websites	• Schedules
• Bank statements	• Invitations	• Search engines
• Brochures	• Labels	• Signs
• Bus schedules	• Letters	• Surveys
• Diagrams	• Manuals	• Television guides
• Directories	• Maps	• Text messages
• Emails	• Memos	• Traffic signs
• Food labels	• Menus	• Warranties
• Game directions	• Pamphlets	• Yellow Pages

What Are Text Features?

Text features are used to help the reader locate and understand information. They are often found in textbooks, magazine articles, web pages, and other forms of informational text. Text features can be divided into three categories: structure, print, and graphics. **Text structure** refers to the way information in the text is organized. The table of contents is a text structure you can find at the beginning of books. **Print features** such as bold words and italics are used to make words stand out in the text. A drawing is an example of a **graphic** aid that can help the reader visualize the text.

	Text Feature	Definition
Structure	Table of Contents	a list of the major parts of a book and the starting page numbers
	Index	an alphabetical list of topics and the page numbers where the information can be found
	Glossary	an alphabetical list of important words with definitions; may include pronunciations
	Appendix	a section at the end of a book that provides additional information
	Heading	the title of the text
	Subheading	a heading given to a section of text
Print	Bold/Color	text printed darker or in color
	Italic	a style of printing where letters slant to the right
	Underlining	a line drawn under the text
	Font	the type and size of the text
	Bullet	a symbol used to emphasize a list of items
	Caption	the words used to explain what is shown in an illustration
Graphics	Illustration	a visual way to give information (examples: photograph, drawing, sketch)
	Sidebar	a boxed section off to the side of the main text that contains related information
	Map	a representation of the earth's surface
	Diagram	a labeled drawing that shows or explains something
	Chart/Table	a graphic organizer used to summarize or compare information
	Timeline	a graphic organizer used to show important events in chronological order
	Graph	a diagram displaying numerical information

Classified Advertisements

Livingston County Press

Lost and Found

FIND Henry! Lost in Storie Subdivision, all white male cat w/stubby tail. $50 reward. Please call 555-333-2527.

PLEASE HELP US find Sheba, female, long-haired, black cat wearing red collar.
Call 555-333-2333 if found.

FOUND: male, yellow lab with faded blue collar, near Mercy Circle Drive. 555-333-4727.

Lost: Glasses in black case on 10/23, in Glenstone Mall. Don't have the money to replace. Call: 555-333-6418

FOUND - Boxer mix, red collar, dragging blue rope, found around Snip 'n Curl. 555-333-0220

Garage Sales

Fri. 14 & Sat. 15, 7- ?
142 Hayward Street
Curio cabinet, pool table, bass boat, clothing, fishing equipment, etc. Items won't last long!

Weird time, cold weather, but awesome sale! Grill, baby clothes, Christmas decorations, furniture, plus lots more! 32 Macon Rd. Sun., 16th, 2-5 pm.

MOVING SALE! 178 Woods Drive, Saturday, 15th from 8-5, girl's clothing (newborn - 5T), women's clothing (all sizes), toys, fireplace insert, futon, mountain sport bicycle, linens, household, Christmas, & misc.

Motorcycles

2006 Road King Classic, one-owner, Black Cherry, lots of chrome, always parked in a garage, less than 2,000 miles, with pull behind trailer. Excellent condition. $16,450 or will consider offer. Call 555-333-2133.

MUST SEE To Appreciate! Model 2004 VTX 1300, black and white, 3K miles. Bought new off show room floor. Owner Must Sell. $4,900 OBO. 555-333-8837

Super bike with lots of extras! 1999 Intruder 800, 19k miles - Unbeatable price of $1,200! Great Bike for Beginner Riders. Call Today! 555-333-6464.

Pets/Pet Supplies

FREE TO GOOD HOME: 6-month-old kitten, black with white on chest, litter box trained. 555-333-6236

FOR SALE - AKC-registered, Cavalier King Charles Spaniel, female, 6 months, current on shots, will make wonderful lap dog. $750.00 Call: 555-333-7455

Want to Place An Ad?
Call: (555) 333-3333
Monday – Friday, 7am – 4pm
Fax: (555) 333-4444
Email:
classified@livngstpress.com
Mail:
P.O. Box 36
Livingston, OK 11111

Include: Name, Address, Phone #, Dates to run, and Payment.

Rate: 25 cents per word

DEADLINE!
Must be submitted by Monday, 2:30 pm, to appear in that week's paper.

Pets/Pet Supplies (cont.)

CUTE and LOVABLE! Beagle dog, 3 years old, neutered, house-broken, great with children. $100. 555-333-8254

AKC Pug Puppies. Very small, 10 weeks old, shots & wormed. $175. Call: 555-333-9527.

10x10 dog pen, chain link, galvanized steel frame $125.
Call: 555-333-8508

ONE AKC registered, female **Saint Bernard** puppy, 11 weeks old, has had first shots. $700. Call: 555-333-7272 (after 5 pm).

For Sale: Friendly, brown dog. Not very old. $100. Call: 555-333-7342.

Classified Advertisements: Practice Activity

Name: _____ **Date:** _____

Practice

Directions: Use the Classified Advertisements document to answer the following questions.

1. What is the street address for the garage sale that advertises a bass boat?

   _____

2. What breed of dog was found on Mercy Circle Drive? _____

3. Under which subheading is the dog pen listed? _____

4. How much does it cost to place a 20-word ad in the newspaper? What is the textual evidence

   that supports your answer? _____

   _____

5. Which words help the reader understand the meaning of **deadline** as used in the "Want to

   Place An Ad?" section in column 3? _____

   _____

Analyze and Evaluate

6. Identify the types of information (age, breed, color, etc.) found in the two advertisements below. Record your findings in the appropriate box.

ADVERTISEMENT #1	ADVERTISEMENT #2
ONE AKC registered, Female **Saint Bernard** puppy, 11 weeks old, has had first shots, $700. Call: 555-333-7272 (after 5 pm).	**For Sale:** Friendly, brown dog. Not very old. $100 Call: 555-333-7342.

7. Based on your findings, which is the better advertisement? Support your answer with details
   from the completed chart.

   _____

   _____

   _____

Email

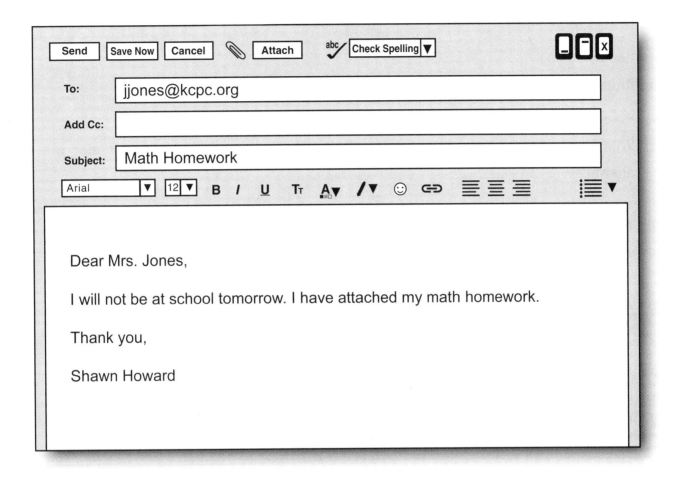

Email Netiquette

1. Include a short title in the Subject line.
2. Open your email with the correct greeting.

   Examples of appropriate greetings: Hi, (informal)

   Dear Mr. Smith, (formal)
3. The message should be short and to the point.
4. Use standard capitalization and spelling.
5. Skip lines between paragraphs.
6. Use CC (Carbon Copy) to send the same message to more than one person at a time. Use BCC (Blind Carbon Copy) to send the same message to more than one person at a time without letting all the recipients see everyone else's email addresses.
6. Avoid fancy fonts and the use of all capital letters.
7. Be sure to type your name at the bottom. Use both first and last names for a formal email.
8. Proofread and use spell check before sending.

Email: Practice Activity

Name: _____ Date: _____

Practice

Directions: Use the Email document to answer the following questions.

1. Who composed the email? _____

2. What document is attached to the email? What is the textual evidence that supports your answer? _____

   _____

3. What text font was used? _____

4. What is the author's purpose for writing the email? _____

   _____

5. Which words help the reader understand the meaning of **appropriate** as used in the "Email Netiquette" section? _____

Apply

Compose an email to Marilyn DeWitt, the mayor of Trenton, requesting tourist information about her city. The mayor's email address is mdewitt@trentoncityhall.gov. Be specific about the types of information you are requesting. Write your email on the screen below.

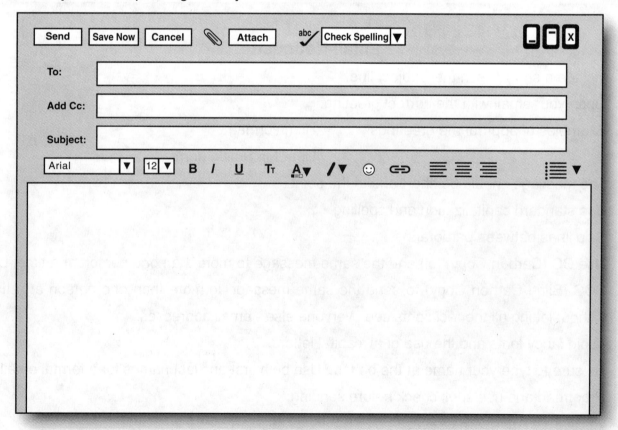

Family Calendar

Sullivan Family Calendar
January

Sunday	Monday	Tuesday	Wednesday	Thursday	Friday	Saturday
		1 New Year's Day (No School)	2 T–Honor Choir 3:30–5:00	3 M–Gymnastics 5:30–6:30 T–History Test	4 M–Bake 3 dozen cookies for bake sale	5 M–Work Bake Sale S–Jill's Birthday Party
6	7 J & S–Karate 4:00–5:30	8 M–Book Report Due	9 S–School Play Tryouts T–Honor Choir 3:30–5:00	10 M–Gymnastics 5:30–6:30	11	12
13	14 J & S–Karate 4:00–5:30	15	16 T–Honor Choir 3:30–5:00	17 M–Gymnastics 5:30–6:30	18 M & J–Turn in Magazine Fundraiser Orders	19 S–Karate Competition, Springfield, 9:00–3:30
20	21 J & S–Karate 4:00–5:30	22	23 T–Honor Choir 3:30–5:00	24 M–Gymnastics 5:30–6:30	25 M, J, T, & S–Family Game Night	26 J–Karate Competition, Springfield, 9:00–3:30
27	28 J & S–Karate 4:00–5:30	29 M–Book Report Due	30 J–Math Test T–Honor Choir 3:30–5:00	31		Children Key: M = Mary T = Teresa J = Jim S = Susan

M & J–Middle-School Magazine Sales Fundraiser

Family Calendar: Practice Activity

Name: _____ **Date:** _____

Practice

Directions: Use the Family Calendar document to answer the following questions.

1. Which child is scheduled to attend Jill's birthday party? _____

2. Which activity does Teresa attend every Wednesday? _____

3. All the children are scheduled to attend which activity? _____

4. Why is January 12 the best Saturday for Mrs. Sullivan to schedule a family night at the movies? What is the textual evidence that supports your answer? _____

    _____

    _____

5. What is the date of Jim's math test? _____

Apply

Fill in the calendar showing your scheduled family activities for a week.

My Family Calendar						
Sunday	**Monday**	**Tuesday**	**Wednesday**	**Thursday**	**Friday**	**Saturday**

Key:

Food Nutrition Labels

A food nutrition label is printed somewhere on the outside of most packaged food. The Food and Drug Administration (FDA) requires the ingredients be listed in order, starting with the most used products to the least used products in the food.

Yum Yum Cereal
Nutrition Facts

Serving Size 3/4 Cup (30 g/1.0 oz.)
Servings Per Container   About 18

Amount Per Serving	Cereal	Cereal with 1/2 cup Vitamins A&D Fat Free Milk
Calories	120	160
Calories from Fat	10	10
	% Daily Value	
Total Fat 0g*	0%	0%
Saturated Fat 0g	0%	0%
Trans Fat 0g		
Cholesterol 0mg	0%	0%
Sodium 150mg	8%	11%
Potassium 75mg	2%	8%
Total Carbohydrates 32g	10%	12%
Dietary Fiber 3g	10%	10%
Sugars 12g		
Other Carbohydrates 17g		
Protein 2g		
Vitamin A	10%	15%
Vitamin C	20%	20%
Calcium	10%	15%
Iron	45%	45%
Thiamin	35%	40%
Riboflavin	35%	45%
Niacin	25%	25%
Vitamin B_6	25%	35%
Folic Acid	25%	25%
Vitamin B_{12}	35%	45%

INGREDIENTS: WHOLE GRAIN WHEAT, SUGAR, SODIUM CHLORIDE, HIGH FRUCTOSE CORN SYRUP, MALT FLAVORING, NATURAL AND ARTIFICIAL FLAVOR.
VITAMINS AND MINERALS: IRON, CALCIUM CARBONATE, NICINAMIDE, ASCORBIC ACID (VITAMIN C), VITAMIN B_6, VITAMIN B_{12}, FOLIC ACID.

Multi Grain Cereal
Nutrition Facts

Serving Size 1 Cup (29 g)
Servings Per Container   About 16

Amount Per Serving	Cereal	Cereal with 1/2 cup Vitamins A&D Fat Free Milk
Calories	110	150
Calories from Fat	10	10
	% Daily Value	
Total Fat 1g*	2%	2%
Saturated Fat 0g	0%	0%
Trans Fat 0g		
Cholesterol 0mg	0%	1%
Sodium 120mg	5%	7%
Potassium 140mg	4%	10%
Total Carbohydrates 24g	8%	10%
Dietary Fiber 3g	10%	10%
Sugars 6g		
Other Carbohydrates 15g		
Protein 2g		
Vitamin A	10%	15%
Vitamin C	10%	10%
Calcium	10%	25%
Iron	45%	45%
Thiamin	25%	30%
Riboflavin	25%	35%
Niacin	25%	25%
Vitamin B_6	25%	25%
Folic Acid	50%	50%
Vitamin B_{12}	25%	35%

INGREDIENTS: WHOLE GRAIN CORN, WHOLE GRAIN OATS, SUGAR, SALT, WHOLE GRAIN BARLEY, NATURAL AND ARTIFICIAL FLAVOR.
VITAMINS AND MINERALS: CALCIUM CARBONATE, ZINC AND IRON, VITAMIN C, VITAMIN B_6, VITAMIN B_{12}, FOLIC ACID.

Food Nutrition Labels: Practice Activity

Name: _____ Date: _____

Practice

Directions: Use the Food Nutrition Label document to answer the following questions.

1. Which cereal has the **most** sugar per serving? What is the textual evidence that supports your answer? _____

   _____

2. Which cereal has the **fewest** calories per serving? _____

3. What is the main ingredient in Multi Grain Cereal? _____

4. How many grams of carbohydrates are in a serving of Yum Yum Cereal? _____

5. Which words help the reader understand the meaning of **ingredients** as used on the food nutrition labels? _____

Analyze and Evaluate

6. Compare the food nutrition labels of three actual breakfast cereals that you have at home or that the teacher brings to class. Record your data in the chart below.

Nutrition Information (per serving)	Cereals		
	Cereal A	**Cereal B**	**Cereal C**
Serving Size			
Calories			
Total Fat			
Cholesterol			
Sodium			
Potassium			
Carbohydrates			
Fiber			
Sugar			
Protein			
Iron			

7. Which of the three cereals is best for a healthy diet? Explain your answer using data from the above chart. _____

   _____

   _____

Internet Search Screen

Home | Start Over | Help | About Us

I-Search

| horses | **Search >>** |

1. **MARYMOUNT FARMS**
Marymount Farms is located in Kentucky. The farm is famous for training race horses. This website provides expert tips on raising horses to race.
www.marymountfarms.com/horsecare

2. **HORSE ASSOCIATION OF THE AMERICAS**
Provides information for horse owners on the benefits of joining a regional riding club. There are links to clubs in the United States, Canada, and Mexico. Membership in this organization includes a monthly e-newsletter.
http://horseaa.org

3. **AKHAL-TEKE HORSES**
These horses were almost extinct in the wild. Breeding programs have worked to increase the number of Akhal-Teke horses. Includes videos, photos, and facts.
www.Animalsrunningwild/Akhal-Teke/preservation.com

4. **WATTS HORSE CAMP AND RANCH**
A week-long camp for girls ages 10–16 who love horses. In addition to daily rides, campers attend classes on horsemanship, horse care, and competitive riding. Includes information about the ranch, weekly class schedule, photos, and a list of items to bring to camp.
www.wattscampandranch.com

5. **HORSES! HORSES! HORSES!**
Everything you ever wanted to know about horses. Includes an alphabetical list of horse breeds. Each breed has a fact page, puzzles, games, photos, and videos. Fun and interesting site for all ages.
www.horseshorseshorses.net

6. **HORSE FACT CARDS**
Fact cards were created by students in Mrs. Smith's sixth-grade science class at Lincoln Middle School. Each card features sections on horse facts, nutrition and diet, photos, and Web links.
www.lms.k12.mo.us/Smith/Science/horsecards.edu

7. **BREEDS OF HORSES**
Includes pictures, maps, and information on many of the different breeds of horses that can be found on six different continents.
http://www.horsebreeds.net

Next > 1 2 3 4 5 6 7 8 ...

Home I About Us I Privacy Policy I How To Search Tips I Help

Internet Search Screen: Practice Activity

Name: _____ **Date:** _____

Practice

Directions: Use the Internet Search Screen document to answer the following questions.

1. Which is the **best** link to click on to learn how to conduct a successful search on I-Search?

   _____

2. What keyword was entered on I-Search? _____

3. What is the URL for "Horses! Horses! Horses!"? _____

4. What is the title of the **best** web link for learning about horses from around the world? What is the textual evidence that supports your answer? _____

   _____

   _____

5. Which words help the reader understand the meaning of the phrase **in the wild** as used in the section about Akhal-Teke Horses? _____

   _____

Analyze and Technology

Enter the same keyword in two different search engines. Compare and contrast the results from the two search engines. Record your findings on the Venn diagram below.

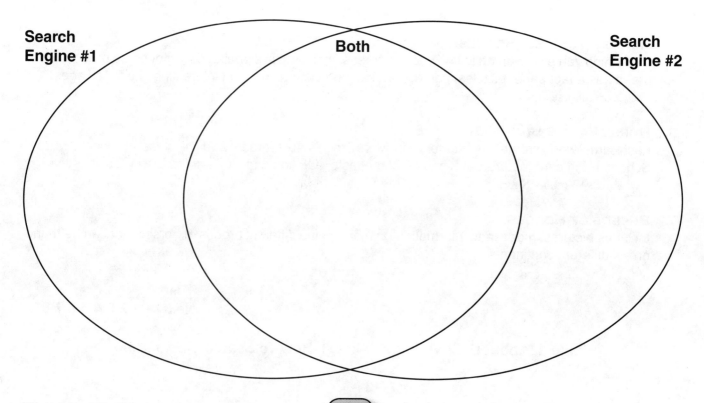

Recipe

Ice Cream in a Bag

Ingredients

1/2 cup milk
1/2 teaspoon vanilla
1 tablespoon sugar
4 cups crushed ice
4 tablespoons salt

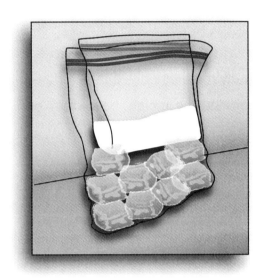

Other materials:
2 quart-size resealable bags,
1 gallon-size resealable bag

Directions

Mix the milk, vanilla and sugar together in a resealable, quart-size bag. Seal tightly, allowing as little air to remain in the bag as possible. Too much air left inside may force the bag to open during shaking. Place this bag inside another resealable, quart-size bag. Again leave as little air inside as possible and seal well. Double-bagging minimizes the risk of salt and ice leaking into the ice cream mixture. This reduces the chance of having salty-tasting ice cream. Put the bagged mixture inside a resealable gallon-size bag. Fill the gallon-size bag with ice, then sprinkle salt on top. Again, let all the air escape and seal the bag. Wrap the bag in a towel. Shake and massage the bag, making sure the ice surrounds the cream mixture. Five to eight minutes is adequate time for the mixture to freeze into ice cream. Serve and enjoy.

Recipe: Practice Activity

Name: _____ **Date:** _____

Practice

Directions: Use the Recipe document to answer the following questions.

1. How many tablespoons of salt are needed to make Ice Cream in a Bag? _____

2. Why is it important to let all the air escape before sealing the bags? _____
_____

3. How many minutes does it take for the mixture to freeze into ice cream? _____

4. If you double the recipe, how many cups of milk would you need? What is the textual evidence that supports your answer? _____
_____

5. Which word helps the reader understand the meaning of **minimizes** as used in the recipe directions? _____

Apply

Create a recipe for a peanut butter and jelly sandwich. Write your recipe on the card.

Recipe for: _____

From the kitchen of: _____

Ingredients:

_____   _____

_____   _____

_____   _____

Directions:

_____

_____

_____

_____

_____

_____

Restaurant Menu

ANTONIO'S PIZZERIA

"FROM OUR OVENS TO YOUR TABLE"

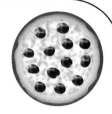

— MENU —

Pizza

	Small (12")	Medium (14")	Large (18")
servings	(1-2)	(2-3)	(4-5)
Cheese	$6.50	$8.50	$10.50
One Topping	$7.50	$9.50	$11.50
Two Toppings	$8.50	$10.50	$12.50
Three Toppings*	$9.50	$11.50	$13.50

*$0.50 for each additional topping

Toppings: pepperoni, hamburger, Canadian bacon, ham, sausage, Italian sausage, chicken, shrimp, bacon, mushrooms, black olives, bell peppers, onions, pineapple, jalapenos, anchovies, spinach, extra cheese

— Specialty Pizzas —
(available only in the 18" size)

Vegetarian: (broccoli, eggplant, tomato, onion, peppers, and mushrooms)................................$12.95
Design Your Own: (2 meats and 3 vegetable toppings)..$14.95
Chicken Alfredo: (chicken, Alfredo sauce, mushrooms, onions, bacon)....................................$13.95
Supreme: (pepperoni, hamburger, sausage, and your choice of veggie toppings)....................$14.95
Dessert: (apple, blueberry, or chocolate chip) $12.95

— Pasta —
(includes salad and bread sticks)

Spaghetti
  w/Marinara Sauce............................$7.95
  w/Meat Sauce..................................$8.95
Manicotti..$9.95

Baked Ravioli...................................$8.95
Chicken Alfredo...............................$9.95
Lasagna..$9.95
Pasta Sampler.................................$10.95

— Soup and Salad —

Homestyle Minestrone........................$3.95

Antipasto Salad..............................$4.95

All drinks $1.00, except water. It's still free!

Restaurant Menu: Practice Activity

Name: _____ Date: _____

Practice

Directions: Use the Restaurant Menu document to answer the following questions.

1. Which food item on the menu costs the **least**? What is the textual evidence that supports your answer? _____

    _____

2. What is the size of a specialty pizza? _____

3. What is the slogan of Antonio's Pizzeria? _____

4. How many servings are in a large pizza? _____

5. What would be the total cost of an 18″ three-topping pizza if you add the additional toppings of onions and shrimp? _____

Apply and Evaluate

6. Use the Restaurant Menu document to place an order. On Guest Check #1, write what you would like to order for a dinner meal. On Guest Check #2, write what you would order for a dinner meal if you only had $10.00 to spend.

GUEST CHECK #1	
Item	**Price**
Subtotal	
Tax (5%)	
Total	

GUEST CHECK #2	
Item	**Price**
Subtotal	
Tax (5%)	
Total	

7. Did the $10 budget affect what you wanted to order? Explain using examples or details.

    _____

    _____

Safety Rules

Safety Rules

Swimming Pool Hours
10:30 a.m. to 11:00 p.m.

- Swimming is allowed only when a lifeguard is on duty.

- Swimmers must follow all instructions of lifeguards.

- Children under the age of 10 must be accompanied by an adult.

- No running or horseplay in shower areas, on pool deck, or concession stand area.

- Dive only in designated areas.

- Food and beverages in concession stand area only.

- Pets are not allowed.

- Be considerate of other swimmers.

- Pool manager reserves the right to deny use of pool to anyone at any time.

Safety Rules: Practice Activity

Name: _____ **Date:** _____

Practice

Directions: Use the Safety Rules document to answer the following questions.

1. Who must be present before you are allowed to swim? What is the textual evidence that supports your answer? _____

   _____

2. An adult must accompany any child under the age of _____.

3. What are the pool hours? _____

4. Where are you allowed to eat a candy bar? _____

5. Which words help the reader understand the meaning of **concession** as used in the sixth rule? _____

   _____

Apply and Evaluate

6. Create four safety rules for your school hallways. Give a reason for each rule.

Hallway Safety Rules	Reason for the Rule
Rule 1:	
Rule 2:	
Rule 3:	
Rule 4:	

7. Which rule do you consider to be the most important? Explain using examples or details.

   _____

   _____

Sales Flyer

Order Your T-shirts and Hoodies Today!

Front   Back

T-shirts $12.00 each and Hoodies $18.00 each

Colors: white/blue (WB) or gray/blue (GB)

Sizes: Youth: Small (YS), Medium (YM), or Large (YL)
Adult: Small (S), Medium (M), Large (L), X-Large (XL), or XX-Large (XXL)

- -

Order Form

Student Name: _____   **Grade:** _____

T-shirts - $12.00 each

Quantity _____   Color (circle one)   WB   GB   Size _____

Quantity _____   Color (circle one)   WB   GB   Size _____

Quantity _____   Color (circle one)   WB   GB   Size _____

Hoodies - $18.00 each

Quantity _____   Color (circle one)   WB   GB   Size _____

Quantity _____   Color (circle one)   WB   GB   Size _____

Quantity _____   Color (circle one)   WB   GB   Size _____

Total Money Enclosed: _____

Reminder: All order forms must be returned to the principal's office by October 15.

Sales Flyer: Practice Activity

Name: _____ **Date:** _____

Practice

Directions: Use the Sales Flyer document to answer the following questions.

1. What is the symbol for the largest adult-sized T-shirt? _____

2. You are purchasing three youth-size T-shirts. On the order form, what amount would you enter for the Total Money Enclosed? _____

3. Order forms must be returned by _____.

4. How many color choices are students given? What is the textual evidence that supports your answer? _____

_____

5. What is the slogan on the T-shirt? _____

Apply

You are a student at Lincoln Middle School. Complete the order form below for the items your family will be ordering. The order is for two large youth-size T-shirts, one in each color; one extra-large adult hoodie in gray/blue; and one medium adult T-shirt in white/blue.

Order Form

Student Name: _____ **Grade:** _____

T-shirts - $12.00 each

Quantity _____ Color (circle one) WB GB Size _____

Quantity _____ Color (circle one) WB GB Size _____

Quantity _____ Color (circle one) WB GB Size _____

Hoodies - $18.00 each

Quantity _____ Color (circle one) WB GB Size _____

Quantity _____ Color (circle one) WB GB Size _____

Quantity _____ Color (circle one) WB GB Size _____

Total Money Enclosed: _____

Reminder: All order forms must be returned to the principal's office by October 15.

Text Message: Practice Activity

Name: _____   **Date:** _____

Results of a recent study showed that over 30 percent of Americans prefer receiving a text message instead of a telephone call. Texting is a form of informal communication. It has its own etiquette and lingo. A text message should be short and simple. The normal length for a text message is 160 characters or less. Using common abbreviations for words or phrases is acceptable.

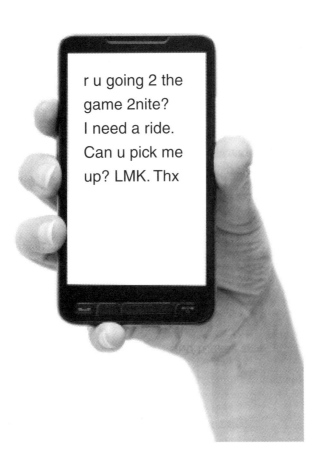

r u going 2 the game 2nite?
I need a ride.
Can u pick me up? LMK. Thx

Commonly Used Text Abbreviations

2 - to
2nite - Tonight
ASAP - As Soon As Possible
BRB - Be Right Back
BTW - By The Way
BFN - Bye For Now
BCNU - Be Seeing You
BFF - Best Friends Forever
ILY - I Love You
L8R - Later
LMK - Let Me Know
POV - Point of View
r - Are
T@UL - Talk At You Later
THX - Thanks
TMI - Too Much Information
TTYL - Talk To You Later
TYVM - Thank You Very Much
UR - You Are

Practice

Apply

1. Rewrite the above text message using standard English. _____

    _____

    _____

    _____

2. Using 160 characters or less, create a text message you could send to a friend.

    _____

    _____

    _____

Learning Stations Activity (Teacher Page)

Title: Understanding a Warranty		
Goal: To provide an opportunity for students to examine and analyze a product warranty.		
Common Core State Standards:		
6th Grade	7th Grade	8th Grade
RL.6.1: Cite textual evidence to support analysis of what the text says explicitly as well as inferences drawn from the text. RL.6.4: Determine the meaning of words and phrases as they are used in a text including figurative, connotative, and technical meanings.	RL.7.1: Cite several pieces of textual evidence to support analysis of what the text says explicitly as well as inferences drawn from the text. RL.7.4: Determine the meaning of words and phrases as they are used in a text including figurative, connotative, and technical meanings; analyze the impact of a specific word choice on meaning or tone.	RL.8.1: Cite the textual evidence that most strongly supports analysis of what the text says explicitly as well as inferences drawn from the text. RL.8.4: Determine the meaning of words and phrases as they are used in a text including figurative, connotative, and technical meanings; analyze the impact of a specific word choice on meaning or tone, including analogies or illusions to other texts.

Materials List/Setup:

Station 1: Warranty and Vocabulary worksheet, one copy per student; dictionaries*

Station 2: Warranty and Real-Life Scenarios worksheet, one copy per student

Station 3: Warranty and Returns worksheet, one copy per student

Station 4: Warranty and Details, Details, Details worksheet, one copy per student

*Technology Integration—Students may choose to use an online dictionary.

Opening: Discussion Questions

Real-World Application: Who has recently purchased an electronic item? What should you do if the item breaks after purchase? What is a warranty? What is the purpose of a warranty? Why should warranty terms be considered when making a purchase?

Student Instructions:

The learning stations will give you the opportunity to examine and analyze a product warranty. You will be working in small groups to complete the worksheet for each station. Before moving to the next station, compare and discuss your answers with the group.

Closure: Reflection Questions

The following questions can be used to stimulate discussion or as a journaling activity.
1. Why is it important for a consumer to understand the terms of a product warranty?
2. Why is it important for a consumer to understand the vocabulary used in a warranty?
3. Why is it important for a consumer to keep proof-of-purchase documentation?

Warranty

One (1) Year Limited Warranty

What does the warranty cover?
For one year from the date of original purchase, this warranty covers failures or defects in the material and/or workmanship of the Horizons television. If a part fails under normal use or conditions, this product will be repaired or exchanged for a similar product. If the product fails within the **first 90 days** after original purchase, return the product to the retailer from which it was purchased for a refund of the purchase price or a product exchange.

Attempts by the consumer to have this product repaired will void this warranty, and Horizons Manufacturing will no longer be responsible for repairs or replacements.

Any product sold as refurbished carries a **ninety day (90) limited warranty**.

Please Note: You are guaranteed certain specific legal rights by this warranty. State laws may provide the consumer with other legal rights.

What is not covered by the warranty?
- damage caused from commercial use
- damage caused from accident, misuse, abuse, or neglect
- shipping and handling charges to return the defective product
- products that were sold "AS IS"
- consumables, such as batteries or fuses
- unauthorized attempts to repair
- failure to operate per the owner's manual
- products used or serviced outside the country of purchase

What to do in case the product needs to be returned:
- Carefully package the television in its original packaging. Return all items, such as remote control and owner's manual.
- Return the product prepaid. It is recommended that you insure the package as any damage caused by shipping is not covered by this warranty.
- Be sure to include a copy of the Warranty Registration Certificate, the original sales slip, and a description of the problem.
- Mail the product to:

    HORIZONS Manufacturing Company
    Attn: Returns Department
    310 N. Randolph Street
    Anytown, USA 78925

What to do if you need product support or additional information?
Visit our company website at www.horizonstelevision.com/customersupport, or you may call 1-555-123-6789.

Station One: Vocabulary

Name: _____ **Date:** _____

Directions: Choose two unfamiliar words from the Warranty document. Complete a graphic organizer for each word.

What words or phrases provide context clues for the meaning of the word?

What do you think this word means? How do you know?

Word

Write the dictionary meaning for the word.

What is the impact or tone of the word as it is used in the document?

What words or phrases provide context clues for the meaning of the word?

What do you think this word means? How do you know?

Word

Write the dictionary meaning for the word.

What is the impact or tone of the word as it is used in the document?

Station Two: Real-Life Scenarios

Name: _____ **Date:** _____

Directions: As a consumer, it is important to know your legal rights under the terms of a warranty. Read each of the scenarios below. Use the Warranty document to answer the questions. Cite text from the Warranty document to support your answers. Share your answers with other group members.

Scenario One:
Mary purchased a Horizons television from a local retail store. Six weeks later, the television stopped working. Mary thought she knew what the problem was and replaced the plug on the end of the cord. The television still did not work.

Question: Is the television still covered by the warranty? **Answer:** (Yes or No)	**How Do You Know?** Cite text from the Warranty document to support your answer.

Scenario Two:
Stephen had saved enough money to purchase a 27″ television. At the store, he decided to buy an "As Is," 40″ television that had been used as a display model. Three days after purchasing the television, it stopped working.

Question: Is the television covered under the warranty? **Answer:** (Yes or No)	**How Do You Know?** Cite text from the Warranty document to support your answer.

Station Three: Returns

Name: _____   **Date:** _____

Directions: Use the Warranty document and the documents below to answer questions about returning a Horizons television.

Burgess Electronics
7595 S. Weller Ave.
Anytown, USA

December 23, 2013

32" Horizons TV	268.95
HDMI Card	32.99
Wall Mount Kit	72.00

Total: $373.94

All Sales Final
See Product Warranty

HORIZONS MANUFACTURING COMPANY
WARRANTY REGISTRATION CERTIFICATE

Thank you for registering your product online.

Purchaser's Name: Mary Cameron
Address: 343 S. Market Street
                              Anytown, USA
Telephone: 111-222-4444
Email: mcameron@sequel.net
Model Number: HR-7500
Serial Number: 7GRGpm39
Purchase Date: 12/23/2013

Please retain this certificate for future warranty claims.

---

1. What is the address for returning a television to Horizons Manufacturing?

   _____

   _____

2. When was the television purchased? _____

3. What is the name of the retail store where the television was purchased?

   _____

4. Who is responsible for paying the cost to return the item?

   _____

5. According to the warranty, what items should also be returned when returning a television to Horizons Manufacturing? _____

   _____

6. What is the model number of the television purchased? _____

7. Who purchased this television? _____

Station Four: Details, Details, Details

Name: _____ **Date:** _____

Directions: It is important for a consumer to understand the terms of a warranty. Use the Warranty document to complete the chart below. Support your answer with textual evidence.

Question	Answer
1. What is the length of the warranty?	
2. What company manufactured the product?	
3. What type of product does the warranty cover?	
4. What is the telephone number to call for product support?	
5. Where do you return the item if it breaks down within the first 90 days?	
6. What action by the consumer can void the warranty?	
7. If a product breaks down under normal use, what actions will the manufacturer take?	
8. If a product breaks down under normal use in the first 90 days, what actions can the retailer take?	
9. Besides the warranty, you may have other legal rights. Who provides these rights?	
10. What are two reasons the warranty will not cover the product?	

Assembly Instructions

Bluebird House Kit

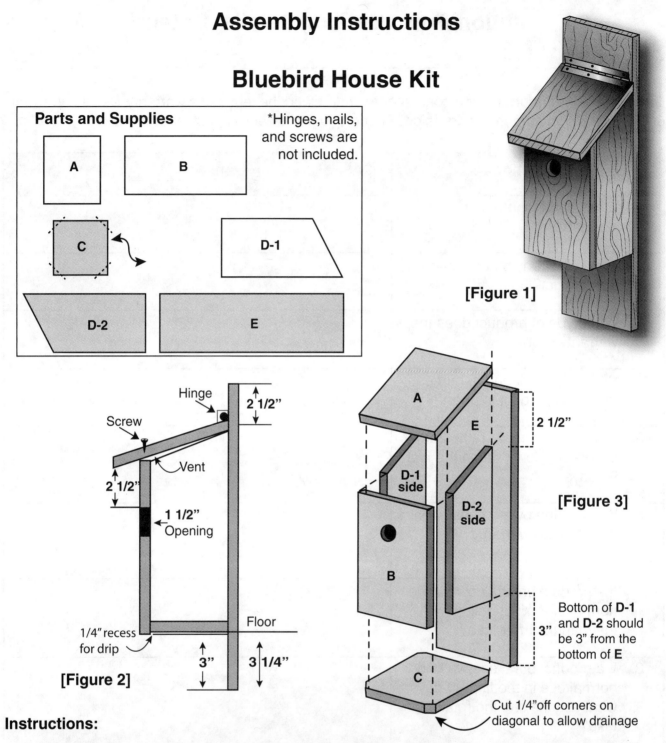

Parts and Supplies

*Hinges, nails, and screws are not included.

A

B

C

D-1

D-2

E

[Figure 1]

[Figure 2]

Hinge

Screw

2 1/2"

Vent

2 1/2"

1 1/2"
Opening

1/4" recess for drip

Floor

3"   3 1/4"

[Figure 3]

A

E

2 1/2"

D-1 side

D-2 side

B

C

Bottom of **D-1** and **D-2** should be 3" from the bottom of **E**

3"

Cut 1/4"off corners on diagonal to allow drainage

Instructions:

1. Use screws or nails to attach part **D-1** and part **D-2** to part **E** [Figure3].

2. Cut $\frac{1}{4}$ inch off each corner of part **C** for drainage [Figure 3].

3. Drill a $1\frac{1}{2}$ inch diameter hole in part **B** [Figure 2].

4. Use screws or nails to attach part **B** to the front edges of **D-1** and **D-2** [Figure 3].

5. Use screws to attach part **C** (floor) to **B**, **D-1**, and **D-2** [Figure 3]. The floor will be flush with the bottom edges of **B**, **D-1**, and **D-2** [Figure 2].

6. Use 2 hinges to attach part **A** to **E** [Figures 2 and 3].

Assembly Instructions: Assessment

Name: _____ **Date:** _____

Directions: Fill in the bubble next to the correct answer for each multiple-choice question.

1. How many parts are included in the kit?
   - ○ a. 2
   - ○ b. 4
   - ○ c. 6
   - ○ d. 8

2. How many inches from the bottom of part E should the floor be placed?
   - ○ a. $3\frac{1}{4}$
   - ○ b. 4
   - ○ c. 3
   - ○ d. $2\frac{1}{2}$

3. The sides are labeled as
   - ○ a. A and E.
   - ○ b. A and B.
   - ○ c. D-1 and D-2.
   - ○ d. C and E.

4. What is the size of the hole that needs to be drilled into part B?
   - ○ a. 1 inch
   - ○ b. $1\frac{1}{2}$ inches
   - ○ c. $2\frac{1}{4}$ inches
   - ○ d. 3 inches

5. Which supplies are not included in the kit?
   - ○ a. nails and screws
   - ○ b. hinges and nails
   - ○ c. screws and hinges
   - ○ d. hinges, nails, and screws

6. What is the purpose for cutting $\frac{1}{4}$ inch off each corner of part C?
   - ○ a. entryway
   - ○ b. drainage
   - ○ c. easy cleaning
   - ○ d. fits better

7. How many hinges are needed to attach part A to part E?
   - ○ a. 1
   - ○ b. 2
   - ○ c. 3
   - ○ d. 4

8. Part A is placed
   - ○ a. 1 inch from the top edge of part E.
   - ○ b. $1\frac{1}{2}$ inches from the opening.
   - ○ c. $2\frac{1}{2}$ inches from the top edge of part E.
   - ○ d. 3 inches from the floor.

9. Drill the opening
   - ○ a. 1 inch from the top edge of part E.
   - ○ b. $1\frac{1}{2}$ inches from the floor.
   - ○ c. $2\frac{1}{2}$ inches from the top edge of part B.
   - ○ d. 3 inches from the floor.

10. The floor is labeled
   - ○ a. C.
   - ○ b. D-1.
   - ○ c. D-2.
   - ○ d. E.

Brochure

Camp Fees and Registration

Early-Bird Registration: Register no later than March 21 (Cost: $589).

Advanced Registration: Register no later than April 23 (Cost: $689).

General Registration: Register no later than June 20 (Cost: $789).

Late Registration: Register no later than July 12 (Cost: $989).

Payment is required at the time of registration.

Contact Information:
CSI Camp
Lake Stockton Science Camp
16795 Hwy E
Grantville, Illinois 75401
222-458-2125 (phone)
csicamp@summerlearning.com

Register online:
www.summerlearning.com/csicamp/reg

Camp Schedule

Monday
Session 1: Steps in Crime Scene Investigation
Session 2: Handwriting Analysis

Tuesday
Session 1: Fingerprint and Shoe Print Lab
Session 2: Mystery Powders Lab

Wednesday
Session 1: DNA Lab
Session 2: Forensic Lab Field Trip

Thursday
Session 1: Case of the Missing Heiress Crime Scene Investigation
Session 2: Case of the Missing Heiress Crime Lab

Friday
Session 1: Solve Case of the Missing Heiress
Session 2: Camp Wrap-up

Each Day
Breakfast: 8:00–9:00 a.m.
Session 1: 9:30–11:30 a.m.
Lunch Break: Noon–1:00 p.m.
Session 2: 1:30–3:30 p.m.
Recreation: 4:00–6:00 p.m. (swimming, canoeing, hiking, and fishing)
Dinner: 6:30–7:30 p.m.
Campfire Activities: 8:00–9:00 p.m.
Lights Out: 10:00 p.m.

CSI Summer Camp

Lake Stockton
July 21–25

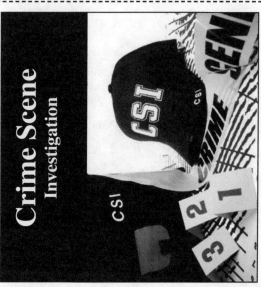

Crime Scene
Investigation

Be part of an unforgettable adventure this summer! Attend CSI Summer Camp at Lake Stockton and become a forensic scientist for a week. You will:

- gather and compare fingerprints and shoe prints.
- test DNA samples.
- learn how to conduct handwriting analysis.
- analyze mystery powders.
- gather clues and test evidence.
- use forensic science to solve a fictional crime.

Brochure: Assessment

Name: _____ **Date:** _____

Directions: Fill in the bubble next to the correct answer for each multiple-choice question.

1. How many days is CSI Camp scheduled?
   - ○ a. 1
   - ○ b. 3
   - ○ c. 5
   - ○ d. 7

2. CSI Camp is located in the state of
   - ○ a. Illinois.
   - ○ b. Indiana.
   - ○ c. Missouri.
   - ○ d. New York.

3. CSI Camp is held in the month of
   - ○ a. May.
   - ○ b. June.
   - ○ c. July.
   - ○ d. August.

4. Which CSI activity is scheduled for Session 2 on Tuesday?
   - ○ a. DNA Lab
   - ○ b. Fingerprint and Shoe Print Lab
   - ○ c. Handwriting Analysis
   - ○ d. Mystery Powders Lab

5. Which registration choice is **least** expensive?
   - ○ a. Early-Bird
   - ○ b. Advanced
   - ○ c. General
   - ○ d. Late

6. What is the **earliest** time breakfast is served?
   - ○ a. 6:00 a.m.
   - ○ b. 7:00 a.m.
   - ○ c. 8:00 a.m.
   - ○ d. 9:00 a.m.

7. What is the total number of camp sessions scheduled?
   - ○ a. 4
   - ○ b. 6
   - ○ c. 8
   - ○ d. 10

8. Which day of camp has a field trip scheduled?
   - ○ a. Monday
   - ○ b. Tuesday
   - ○ c. Wednesday
   - ○ d. Thursday

9. The last registration date for CSI Camp is
   - ○ a. March 21.
   - ○ b. April 23.
   - ○ c. June 20.
   - ○ d. July 12.

10. Which recreational activity is not offered to campers?
    - ○ a. canoeing
    - ○ b. golfing
    - ○ c. hiking
    - ○ d. swimming

Bus Schedule

Bus Schedule

Fares	Full	Reduced
Regular Bus	$1.10	$0.55
Express Bus (EB)	$2.50	$1.25

Weekly Service to Lake View Mall—Red Route				
W Pine/146th St Stop A	Parkway/136th St Stop B	Lincoln/122 St. Stop C	Market/110 St. Stop D*	Lake View Mall Stop E
AM Service (Departure)				**Arrival**
	5:42	5:46	5:50	6:00
7:00	7:12	7:16	7:20	7:30
9:30	9:42	9:46	9:50	10:00
11:00	11:12	11:16	11:20	11:30
PM Service (Departure)				**Arrival**
Noon (EB)				12:12
1:30	1:42	1:46	1:50	2:00
2:00	2:12	2:16	2:20	2:30
3:30	3:42	3:46	3:50	4:00
4:00	4:12	4:16	4:20	4:30
5:30	5:42	5:46	5:50	6:00
6:00	6:12	6:16	6:20	6:30
7:30	7:42	7:46	7:50	8:00

*Bus does not stop on Sundays and holidays.

Discounts

Seniors citizens, riders with limited mobility, and children (ages 5–11) can ride the bus service from 9 a.m.–3 p.m. weekdays for $0.25 and all day on weekends for free (w/ID).

Transfer Slips

Bus transfer slips must be requested when boarding the bus.

Note: Have the exact change or pass ready when you board the bus. This helps to keep the bus on schedule.

Monthly Pass
$30.00

A monthly pass is good for unlimited rides on all regular and express bus service for the month indicated on the pass.

One-Day Pass
$4.00

The pass is good for unlimited rides on all regular and express bus service for the one day indicated on the pass. A pass will be activated the first time the passenger boards the bus.

Bus Schedule: Assessment

Name: _____ Date: _____

Directions: Fill in the bubble next to the correct answer for each multiple-choice question.

1. The bus schedule shows the weekly service to
   - ○ a. the lake.
   - ○ b. Metro City.
   - ○ c. Lake View Mall.
   - ○ d. Metro City Mall.

2. What is the price of a one-day pass?
   - ○ a. $4.00
   - ○ b. $6.50
   - ○ c. $15.00
   - ○ d. $30.00

3. What time does the Express Bus leave Stop A?
   - ○ a. 10:00 a.m.
   - ○ b. 11:00 a.m.
   - ○ c. Noon
   - ○ d. 1:00 p.m.

4. You are 10 years old. How much will it cost to ride the bus at 1:00 p.m. on Tuesday?
   - ○ a. $0.25
   - ○ b. $1.10
   - ○ c. $2.50
   - ○ d. $4.00

5. If you leave the Lincoln/122 St. bus stop at 4:16 p.m., when will you arrive at Market and 110th Street?
   - ○ a. 5:50 p.m.
   - ○ b. 2:00 p.m.
   - ○ c. 3:42 p.m.
   - ○ d. 4:20 p.m.

6. The Market/110th Street bus does not operate on
   - ○ a. Thursday.
   - ○ b. Friday.
   - ○ c. Saturday.
   - ○ d. Sunday.

7. What is the latest time you can leave Stop A to arrive by 10:30 a.m. at the Lake View Mall?
   - ○ a. 5:42 a.m.
   - ○ b. 7:00 a.m.
   - ○ c. 9:30 a.m.
   - ○ d. 11:00 a.m.

8. How much is the reduced fare for the Express Bus?
   - ○ a. $0.25
   - ○ b. $1.25
   - ○ c. $2.50
   - ○ d. $4.00

9. Senior citizens can ride the bus for free
   - ○ a. at 4:00 p.m. on Monday.
   - ○ b. at 7:42 p.m. every day.
   - ○ c. all day on the weekends.
   - ○ d. with a monthly pass.

10. Why is it important to have the exact change ready when you board the bus?
    - ○ a. Some buses do not run on Sundays.
    - ○ b. It helps keep the bus on schedule.
    - ○ c. Regular bus fares are $1.10.
    - ○ d. A monthly pass is good for unlimited rides.

Calendar of Events

Lincoln Middle School
Calendar of Events

Band Camp	August 6–10
Teacher In-Service	August 13–14
Open House	August 14
First Day of School	**August 15**
Spirit Week (All Sports)	August 27–31
Labor Day (No School)	**September 3**
Midway Invitational VB Tournament	September 13–15
School Pictures	September 18
All-School Fundraiser	October 8–12
Parent-Teacher Conference (3:30 p.m.–7:00 p.m.)	October 25–26
6th Grade Carnival	October 30
Thanksgiving Break (No School)	**November 21–23**
Picture Retakes	November 27
Big 8 Conference Basketball Tournament	December 10–14
Christmas Program—6th Grade	December 20
Christmas Vacation (No School)	**December 21–January 1**
School Resumes	January 2
Teacher In-Service (No School)	**January 18**
Honor Society Cookie Dough Sales	January 22–25
Big 8 Conference Honor Choir Tryouts	February 1
Big 8 Conference Honor Choir Program	February 8
Student Art Show	February 13
Library Book Fair	February 18–22
Regional Spelling Bee	March 7
Band/Choir Spring Concert	March 15
School Play	April 4–5
Spring Break (No School)	**April 8–12**
Achievement Test (All-School)	April 22–25
Big 8 Conference Track Meet	April 30
Science Fair—7th and 8th Grade	May 3
8th Grade Class Trip	May 11
Final Exams	May 13–15
School Dance (7:00 p.m.–9:00 p.m.)	May 17
Awards Day	May 23
Last Day of School (Dismiss at Noon)	**May 24**
8th Grade Promotion (1:30 p.m.)	May 24

Calendar of Events: Assessment

Name: _____ Date: _____

Directions: Fill in the bubble next to the correct answer for each multiple-choice question.

1. When is the first day of school?
   - ○ a. August 14
   - ○ b. August 15
   - ○ c. September 3
   - ○ d. September 18

2. The book fair will be held in the month of
   - ○ a. February.
   - ○ b. March.
   - ○ c. October.
   - ○ d. December.

3. For how many hours will the school dance be held?
   - ○ a. 1
   - ○ b. 2
   - ○ c. 3
   - ○ d. 4

4. Which event takes place on September 18?
   - ○ a. 8th Grade Class Trip
   - ○ b. Picture Retakes
   - ○ c. Science Fair
   - ○ d. School Pictures

5. The Regional Spelling Bee will be held in the month of
   - ○ a. January.
   - ○ b. February.
   - ○ c. March.
   - ○ d. April.

6. Which event is being held on December 10–14?
   - ○ a. School Pictures
   - ○ b. Thanksgiving Break
   - ○ c. Student Art Show
   - ○ d. Big 8 Conference Basketball Tournament

7. Which grade will hold their Christmas Program on December 20?
   - ○ a. 5th
   - ○ b. 6th
   - ○ c. 7th
   - ○ d. 8th

8. What item is the Honor Society selling from January 22–25?
   - ○ a. Cookie Dough
   - ○ b. Magazines
   - ○ c. Pizza
   - ○ d. T-shirts

9. Which grade(s) will be competing in the Science Fair?
   - ○ a. 5th and 6th grades
   - ○ b. 7th and 8th grades
   - ○ c. 6th, 7th, and 8th grades
   - ○ d. 8th grade only

10. The school play will be held on how many nights?
    - ○ a. 1
    - ○ b. 2
    - ○ c. 3
    - ○ d. 4

Class Schedule

Eighth Grade Class Schedule—1st Semester							
Student: **Sarah Ripley**			Homeroom Teacher: Mrs. McBaine			Homeroom: 275	
Period	Time	Room	Monday	Tuesday	Wednesday	Thursday	Friday
1	8:10-9:10	275	Science	Science	Science	Science	Science Lab
2	9:15-10:05	283	Writing & Composition	Writing & Composition	Writing & Composition	Writing & Composition	Writing & Composition
3	10:10-11:00	276	Art	Art	Art	Art	Art
4	11:05-11:55	281	Algebra	Algebra	Algebra	Algebra	Algebra
Lunch	11:55-12:20	Cafeteria	Lunch	Lunch	Lunch	Lunch	Lunch
5	12:25-1:15	279	American History	American History	American History	American History	American History
6	1:20-2:10	282	P. E.	P. E.	P. E.	P. E.	P.E.
7	2:15-3:05	287	Spanish II	Spanish II	Spanish II	Spanish II	Spanish II

Eighth Grade Class Schedule—2nd Semester							
Student: **Sarah Ripley**			Homeroom Teacher: Mrs. McBaine			Homeroom: 275	
Period	Time	Room	Monday	Tuesday	Wednesday	Thursday	Friday
1	8:10-9:10	275	Science	Science	Science	Science	Science Lab
2	9:15-10:05	Computer Lab	Computer	Computer	Computer	Computer	Computer
3	10:10-11:00	284	Reading	Reading	Reading	Reading	Reading
4	11:05-11:55	281	Algebra	Algebra	Algebra	Algebra	Algebra
Lunch	11:55-12:20	Cafeteria	Lunch	Lunch	Lunch	Lunch	Lunch
5	12:25-1:15	285	Choir	Choir	Choir	Choir	Choir
6	1:20-2:10	279	American History	American History	American History	American History	American History
7	2:15-3:05	287	Spanish II	Spanish II	Spanish II	Spanish II	Spanish II

Class Schedule: Assessment

Name: _____ **Date:** _____

Directions: Fill in the bubble next to the correct answer for each multiple-choice question.

1. Which class is only scheduled for 2nd semester?
    - ○ a. Science
    - ○ b. Computer
    - ○ c. Algebra
    - ○ d. American History

2. In order to take Spanish II, we can assume a student has already taken
    - ○ a. French I.
    - ○ b. Writing & Composition.
    - ○ c. Spanish I.
    - ○ d. Reading.

3. Which class is not scheduled for the same time period both semesters?
    - ○ a. Spanish II
    - ○ b. Science
    - ○ c. American History
    - ○ d. Algebra

4. Art is scheduled
    - ○ a. 1st semester at 10:10-11:00.
    - ○ b. 1st semester at 12:25-1:15.
    - ○ c. 2nd semester at 10:10-11:00.
    - ○ d. 2nd semester at 12:25-1:15.

5. Choir is held in Room
    - ○ a. 275.
    - ○ b. 276.
    - ○ c. 285.
    - ○ d. 287.

6. Who is the homeroom teacher?
    - ○ a. Ms. Evans
    - ○ b. Mr. Senninger
    - ○ c. Mr. Hepler
    - ○ d. Mrs. McBaine

7. Where do students go after Algebra?
    - ○ a. P. E.
    - ○ b. Lunch
    - ○ c. Art
    - ○ d. Reading

8. The class schedules are for
    - ○ a. Dianne Wallace.
    - ○ b. Molly Williams.
    - ○ c. John Grant.
    - ○ d. Sarah Ripley.

9. The class schedules are for a student in grade
    - ○ a. five.
    - ○ b. six.
    - ○ c. seven.
    - ○ d. eight.

10. Which subject has a scheduled lab?
    - ○ a. Science
    - ○ b. Reading
    - ○ c. P. E.
    - ○ d. Spanish II

Game Rules

Checkers

Checkers is a game for two players. It is played on a standard game board consisting of 64 squares. The squares are colored in alternating red and black. Each player receives 12 checkers of all black or red. The game board is placed in the center, and the players sit on opposite sides, facing each other.

[Figure 1]

How do you set up a game board?

Players place their checkers on the black squares in the three rows closest to them [Figure 1].

Who moves first?

For the first game, the player with the black checkers moves first. The winner moves first in the succeeding game.

How do you move the checkers?

Players move their checkers forward one square in a diagonal direction [Figure 2]. The square must be "open," which means it is not occupied by another checker. After taking a turn, play alternates to the other player.

[Figure 2]

How do you capture or jump the opposing player's checkers?

There have to be two conditions for a capture or jump to happen. First, a player's checker has to be next to the opposing player's checker. Second, there has to be an open square on the other side of this checker. A player must jump the checker and land in the open space. The player has captured the opposing player's checker and removes it from the board. If a jump leads to another jump, the player <u>must</u> take the multiple jumps [Figure 3].

How do you crown a king?

When a player's checker reaches the first row of the opposing player, the checker becomes a king. To signify the checker being kinged or crowned, the checker will be turned over revealing the crown side. Another method is to place a second checker on top of the original checker. The second checker is a captured piece of the same color.

How does a king checker move?

A king checker moves one square in a diagonal direction; however, unlike a regular checker, it can move forward or backward.

[Figure 3]

How do you determine the winner of the game?

The first player to capture all the checkers of the opposing player or completely block the opposing player from making a move wins the game.

Game Rules: Assessment

Name: _____ **Date:** _____

Directions: Fill in the bubble next to the correct answer for each multiple-choice question.

1. Checkers is a game for how many players?
   - ○ a. 1
   - ○ b. 2
   - ○ c. 3
   - ○ d. 4

2. In the first game of checkers, which player moves first?
   - ○ a. player with the black checkers
   - ○ b. player with the red checkers
   - ○ c. player with the white checkers
   - ○ d. player with the green checkers

3. Checkers move forward one square in which direction?
   - ○ a. horizontal
   - ○ b. diagonal
   - ○ c. vertical
   - ○ d. perpendicular

4. When a player's checker reaches the front row of the opposing player, the checker becomes a
   - ○ a. winner.
   - ○ b. loser.
   - ○ c. king.
   - ○ d. queen.

5. How does a king checker differ from a regular checker?
   - ○ a. The king can move forward or backward in a diagonal direction.
   - ○ b. The king can make multiple jumps.
   - ○ c. The king can only capture other king checkers.
   - ○ d. The king can move forward or backward in a horizontal direction.

6. How can you identify a king checker?
   - ○ a. A king checker is two stacked checkers of the same color.
   - ○ b. A king checker is yellow.
   - ○ c. A king checker is a black checker with a red checker stacked on top.
   - ○ d. A king checker is a red checker with a black checker stacked on top.

7. If a jump leads to another jump, the player
   - ○ a. must take the jump.
   - ○ b. can decide to pass.
   - ○ c. can chose not to take the jump.
   - ○ d. must forfeit the game.

8. How many squares are on a standard game board?
   - ○ a. 24
   - ○ b. 36
   - ○ c. 48
   - ○ d. 64

9. In order for a checker to move into another square, the square must be
   - ○ a. occupied.
   - ○ b. open.
   - ○ c. captured.
   - ○ d. blocked.

10. When a player has captured the opposing player's checker, the captured checker is
   - ○ a. traded for another checker.
   - ○ b. returned to its home position.
   - ○ c. turned into a king checker.
   - ○ d. removed from the board.

Mall Directory

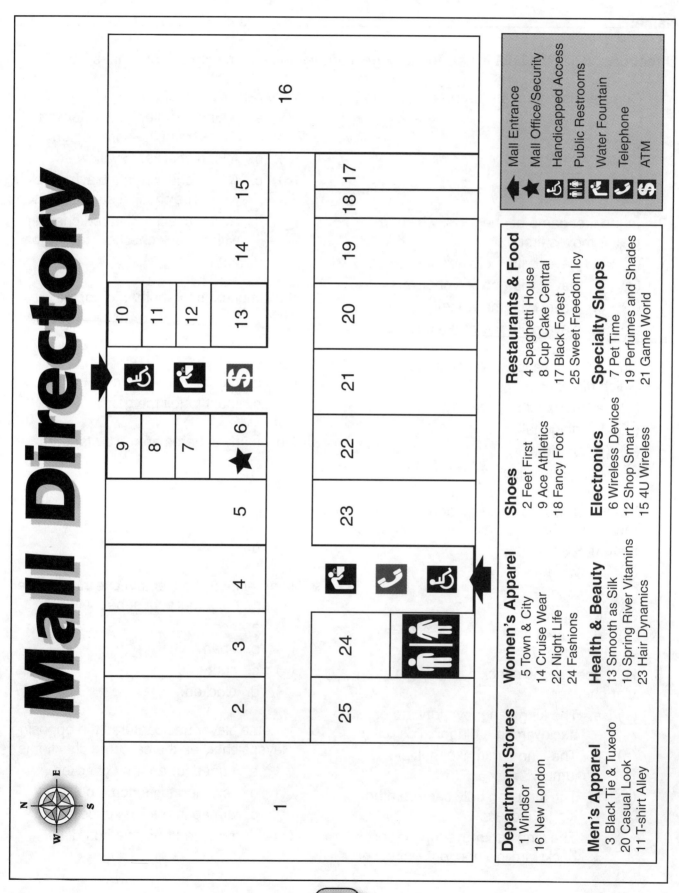

Department Stores
1 Windsor
16 New London

Men's Apparel
3 Black Tie & Tuxedo
20 Casual Look
11 T-shirt Alley

Women's Apparel
5 Town & City
14 Cruise Wear
22 Night Life
24 Fashions

Health & Beauty
13 Smooth as Silk
10 Spring River Vitamins
23 Hair Dynamics

Shoes
2 Feet First
9 Ace Athletics
18 Fancy Foot

Electronics
6 Wireless Devices
12 Shop Smart
15 4U Wireless

Restaurants & Food
4 Spaghetti House
8 Cup Cake Central
17 Black Forest
25 Sweet Freedom Icy

Specialty Shops
7 Pet Time
19 Perfumes and Shades
21 Game World

Mall Entrance
Mall Office/Security
Handicapped Access
Public Restrooms
Water Fountain
Telephone
ATM

Mall Directory: Assessment

Name: _____ Date: _____

Directions: Fill in the bubble next to the correct answer for each multiple-choice question.

1. How many stores are listed on the Mall Directory?
   - ○ a. 8
   - ○ b. 14
   - ○ c. 20
   - ○ d. 25

2. Which heading would you look under to find a store that sold cell phones?
   - ○ a. Department Stores
   - ○ b. Electronics
   - ○ c. Health and Beauty
   - ○ d. Specialty Shops

3. Where is the public telephone located?
   - ○ a. east entrance
   - ○ b. west entrance
   - ○ c. north entrance
   - ○ d. south entrance

4. Which restaurant is located between the Black Tie & Tuxedo store and Town & City store?
   - ○ a. Black Forest
   - ○ b. Cup Cake Central
   - ○ c. Spaghetti House
   - ○ d. Sweet Freedom Icy

5. Which shop is closest to the public restrooms?
   - ○ a. Cruise Wear
   - ○ b. Hair Dynamics
   - ○ c. Perfume and Shades
   - ○ d. 4U Wireless

6. Which store would be a good place to shop for a pair of running shoes?
   - ○ a. 6
   - ○ b. 9
   - ○ c. 11
   - ○ d. 12

7. Which store is closest to the ATM machine?
   - ○ a. 13
   - ○ b. 16
   - ○ c. 19
   - ○ d. 24

8. Which store is labeled 21 on the mall map?
   - ○ a. Game World
   - ○ b. New London
   - ○ c. Shop Smart
   - ○ d. Spring River Vitamins

9. The star indicates the location of the
   - ○ a. public restrooms.
   - ○ b. mall entrance.
   - ○ c. mall office/security.
   - ○ d. water fountain.

10. Which store would carry supplies for your cat?
    - ○ a. Feet First
    - ○ b. Pet Time
    - ○ c. Shop Smart
    - ○ d. Smooth as Silk

Movie Guide

HOLLYWOOD CINEMA
231 South Vine (111-555-SHOW)
Purchase Tickets Online at:
hollywoodcinema.com

BARBARIANS AT THE GATE (R)
4:05 7: 15 9:45
THE DAY THE EARTH DANCED (G)
3:55 7:00 9:20
WATCH ME RUN (PG)
5:35 6:25 8:35

EVERY SEAT $2.00

SPRINGFIELD THEATERS

812 West Montclair
111-555-2354

Visit www.springfieldtheatersmovies.com
for details and ticket price

NOW SHOWING IN 3D:
EXTREME SKATEBOARDING (G)
3:40 5:50 7:55 9:25
THE KID (G)
1:30 4:40 7:25 9:45
PEAK (PG)
2:05 4:15 6:45 8:35 10:00
CRY BABY CRY (R)
9:40
WEDDING DISASTERS (R)
3:40 5:50 7:55 9:25
SHIPWRECK (PG-13)
12:40 2:50 4:55 6:15
RELEASING THE TIGER (PG)
1:30 3:40 5:35 7:25

Child $5.50   Student $6.75
Adult $8.75   Senior $7.00

DIGITAL SOUND AND STADIUM SEATING
Assistive Listening Devices Available

CINEMA 9
107 South Avenue
(111-55M-OVIE)

Bargain Matinees Daily
(Before 6 p.m.)

THE REVENGE OF THE VIPERS (PG-13)
1:30 4:40 7:25 9:45
■ **GO CRAZY!** (R)
1:30 4:40 7:25 9:45
ON THE WAY WEST (PG)
2:30 5:30 8:25 10:05
COUGAR MOUNTAIN (G)
3:40 5:50 7:55 9:25
CRY BABY CRY (R)
5:40 7:50 9:55
ONWARD TO GLORY (G)
2:40 4:50 7:00 10:25
VICTORY FOR ALL (R)
5:50 7:55 9:25
RISING OF THE MOON (PG)
2:20 5:30 7:25 9:15
BURNING BRIDGES (PG-13)
1:40 3:45 7:05 9:00

HALF OFF MONDAYS
ALL SHOWS - ALL TICKETS

Buy Lg. Popcorn and
Drink Combo for $8

Refills Free

■ No Passes

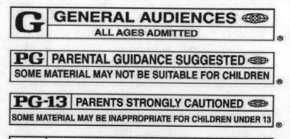

Movie Guide: Assessment

Name: _____ Date: _____

Directions: Fill in the bubble next to the correct answer for each multiple-choice question.

1. The purpose of a movie guide is to
   - ○ a. advertise the snack bar.
   - ○ b. display the movie theater rules.
   - ○ c. list movies and showtimes.
   - ○ d. promote award-winning movies.

2. The movie *Shipwreck* is showing at
   - ○ a. Cinema 9.
   - ○ b. Film Festival.
   - ○ c. Hollywood Cinema.
   - ○ d. Springfield Theaters.

3. Which movie is showing in 3D?
   - ○ a. *Barbarians at the Gate*
   - ○ b. *Extreme Skateboarding*
   - ○ c. *Peak*
   - ○ d. *The Day the Earth Danced*

4. Which theatre allows a moviegoer to purchase tickets online?
   - ○ a. Cinema 9
   - ○ b. Film Festival
   - ○ c. Hollywood Cinema
   - ○ d. Springfield Theaters

5. Which movie requires anyone under the age of 17 to be accompanied by a parent or adult guardian?
   - ○ a. *Go Crazy!*
   - ○ b. *Rising of the Moon*
   - ○ c. *Shipwreck*
   - ○ d. *Watch Me Run*

6. Which theater offers bargain matinees?
   - ○ a. Cinema 9
   - ○ b. Film Festival
   - ○ c. Hollywood Cinema
   - ○ d. Springfield Theaters

7. The movie rating PG stands for
   - ○ a. general audiences.
   - ○ b. parental guidance suggested.
   - ○ c. parents strongly cautioned.
   - ○ d. restricted.

8. How much is a student ticket for the movie *Peak*?
   - ○ a. $2.00
   - ○ b. $5.50
   - ○ c. $6.75
   - ○ d. $8.75

9. Which movie is showing at two theaters?
   - ○ a. *Barbarians at the Gate*
   - ○ b. *Cougar Mountain*
   - ○ c. *Cry Baby Cry*
   - ○ d. *Releasing The Tiger*

10. What is the **earliest** showtime for *Revenge of the Vipers*?
    - ○ a. 1:30
    - ○ b. 4:40
    - ○ c. 7:25
    - ○ d. 9:45

Permission Letter

Dear Parent/Guardian:

On January 17, the sixth-grade class will take a field trip to the Newport Science Museum. Eighty-eight percent of my students chose the Newport Science Museum as their favorite place to visit. The museum has hands-on science exhibits and activities for children of all ages. The following exhibits are highlighted in the museum's brochure.

- Outer Space—Experience the beauty of outer space in a 110-seat planetarium. Sit back, relax, and enjoy this incredible journey through our solar system.

- Science Learning Lab—Become a scientist. Conduct experiments using the scientific method. Put on a lab coat and get ready to have fun while learning!

- Wings and Things—Explore the four basic principles of flight. Design a paper airplane, make a rocket, or climb into a cockpit simulator.

- Dino Digs—Journey back into prehistoric times through this multi-station exhibit. Become a member of an expedition team and experience a hands-on dig.

I feel the museum is an excellent choice for a field trip. It will be a great way to review topics we have explored in our science class. The hands-on exhibits will hold the students' interest. It is a short bus ride from the school.

Students will need to bring a sack lunch, snack, and drink. They should wear comfortable clothing. The $2.00 admission fee will be paid by the Parent Teacher Organization. Students will not be allowed to purchase souvenirs.

Please let me know if you have any questions. The permission slip below must be returned to me by January 10.

Mrs. Jones

- -

_____ has my permission to attend the sixth-grade
(Student Name)

field trip to the Newport Science Museum.

_____
Parent/Guardian Signature

Permission Letter: Assessment

Name: _____ **Date:** _____

Directions: Fill in the bubble next to the correct answer for each multiple-choice question.

1. What is the main purpose of the letter?
   - ○ a. to entertain
   - ○ b. to inform
   - ○ c. to describe
   - ○ d. to persuade

2. Which exhibit would a student visit to learn more about the moon?
   - ○ a. Outer Space
   - ○ b. Science Learning Lab
   - ○ c. Wings and Things
   - ○ d. Dino Digs

3. Why does Mrs. Jones believe the Newport Science Museum is a good choice for a field trip?
   - ○ a. students can bring a sack lunch
   - ○ b. great way to review science topics
   - ○ c. souvenirs cannot be purchased
   - ○ d. admission fee will be paid

4. Which organizational feature is used to list the museum exhibits?
   - ○ a. boldface print
   - ○ b. bullets
   - ○ c. diagrams
   - ○ d. italics

5. Which exhibit features a cockpit simulator?
   - ○ a. Outer Space
   - ○ b. Science Learning Lab
   - ○ c. Wings and Things
   - ○ d. Dino Digs

6. The permission slip is to be returned by
   - ○ a. January 7.
   - ○ b. January 10.
   - ○ c. January 17.
   - ○ d. January 20.

7. The percentage of students who selected the Newport Science Museum as their favorite place to visit is
   - ○ a. 17.
   - ○ b. 54.
   - ○ c. 72.
   - ○ d. 88.

8. Which grade does Mrs. Jones teach?
   - ○ a. 4
   - ○ b. 5
   - ○ c. 6
   - ○ d. 7

9. Which exhibit allows you to explore the scientific method?
   - ○ a. Outer Space
   - ○ b. Science Learning Lab
   - ○ c. Wings and Things
   - ○ d. Dino Digs

10. On the field trip, students were told to bring
    - ○ a. a sack lunch.
    - ○ b. a camera.
    - ○ c. the admission fee.
    - ○ d. the money for souvenirs.

Poster

BE A GERM FIGHTER!

Germs cause disease. You can't see germs, but they are on everything you touch. The single most important thing you can do to fight the spread of germs at school is to wash your hands.

Wash your hands
- after using the bathroom.
- after coughing or sneezing.
- after touching books and money.
- before eating.

Hand Washing Steps

Step 1: Wet your hands with warm water.

Step 2: Lather both hands with soap for 20 seconds.

Step 3: Wash between fingers, wrists, under fingernails, and the back of your hands.

Step 4: Rinse the soap from your hands.

Step 5: Dry your hands with a clean paper towel.

Step 6: Turn off the water using a paper towel.

Note: If soap and water are not available, use alcohol-based hand sanitizer.

Poster: Assessment

Name: _____   **Date:** _____

Directions: Fill in the bubble next to the correct answer for each multiple-choice question.

1. What is the most important thing you can do to stop the spread of germs?
   - ○ a. do not touch door knobs
   - ○ b. sneeze into a Kleenex
   - ○ c. cover mouth when coughing
   - ○ d. hand washing

2. When washing your hands, what is a good substitute for soap and water?
   - ○ a. alcohol-based hand sanitizer
   - ○ b. bleach and cold water
   - ○ c. hand lotion
   - ○ d. first aid cream

3. Which step comes immediately after rinsing the soap from your hands?
   - ○ a. 1
   - ○ b. 3
   - ○ c. 5
   - ○ d. 6

4. What does the poster recommend doing before turning off the water?
   - ○ a. Wet your hands.
   - ○ b. Lather both hands.
   - ○ c. Rinse your hands.
   - ○ d. Dry your hands.

5. Why are you instructed to use a paper towel to turn off the water?
   - ○ a. The knob has germs on it.
   - ○ b. The knob might be hot.
   - ○ c. The paper towel will keep the knob clean.
   - ○ d. The paper towel will help you turn the knob off.

6. In which step are you directed to wash under your fingernails?
   - ○ a. 2
   - ○ b. 3
   - ○ c. 4
   - ○ d. 5

7. According to the poster, why is it important to wash your hands?
   - ○ a. Hands get dirty at school.
   - ○ b. Your hands will smell better.
   - ○ c. Germs are everywhere.
   - ○ d. Hand washing gets rid of dead skin cells.

8. Germs cause
   - ○ a. allergies.
   - ○ b. disease.
   - ○ c. headaches.
   - ○ d. obesity.

9. According to the poster, how many seconds should you lather your hands?
   - ○ a. 10
   - ○ b. 20
   - ○ c. 30
   - ○ d. 40

10. How many hand-washing steps are listed on the poster?
    - ○ a. 6
    - ○ b. 7
    - ○ c. 8
    - ○ d. 9

School Lunch Menu

George Washington Carver Middle School
September Lunch Menu

Monday	Tuesday	Wednesday	Thursday	Friday
5 No School Labor Day * Total calories of entire meal with skim milk	**6** Fiesta Fajitas *680 Grilled Chicken, Soft Flour Tortillas, Cheese, and Salsa Spanish Rice Grilled Veggies **Watermelon Slice Ice Cold Milk	**7** Soup & Sandwich *610 Grilled Cheese Sandwich on Wheat Bread Creamy Tomato Soup w/Saltine Crackers Orange Wedges Ice Cold Milk	**8** Italian Pizza Pie *715 Homemade Pepperoni Pizza Fresh Carrot Sticks w/Low-Fat Dip Pineapple Chunks Ice Cold Milk	**9** Chuck Wagon *975 BBQ Pork Rib on Wheat Bun Oven Fries Baked Beans Apple Crisp Ice Cold Milk

What's For Lunch?

Meal Payment Guidelines: There is no charging for any meals without approval of the office.

**MENU SUBJECT TO CHANGE

LUNCH PRICES (includes milk)

Students	$1.75
Reduced	$0.40
Adult	$3.75
Milk	$0.25
Types:	
skim	80 calories
2%	120 calories
lowfat chocolate	158 calories

School Lunch Menu: Assessment

Name: _____ **Date:** _____

Directions: Fill in the bubble next to the correct answer for each multiple-choice question.

1. A student lunch with an additional milk costs
   - ○ a. $1.75.
   - ○ b. $2.00.
   - ○ c. $2.25.
   - ○ d. $2.50.

2. The total calories of each meal includes a serving of
   - ○ a. skim milk.
   - ○ b. 2% milk.
   - ○ c. lowfat chocolate milk.
   - ○ d. whole milk.

3. Which item on the menu is subject to change?
   - ○ a. carrots
   - ○ b. fries
   - ○ c. salsa
   - ○ d. watermelon

4. Lunch will not be served on
   - ○ a. Monday.
   - ○ b. Tuesday.
   - ○ c. Wednesday.
   - ○ d. Friday.

5. Which meal has a total calorie count of 715?
   - ○ a. Fiesta Fajitas
   - ○ b. Soup & Sandwich
   - ○ c. Italian Pizza Pie
   - ○ d. Chuck Wagon

6. Meal charges must be approved by the
   - ○ a. cook.
   - ○ b. cashier.
   - ○ c. dietitian.
   - ○ d. office.

7. The School Lunch Menu is for the month of
   - ○ a. September.
   - ○ b. October.
   - ○ c. November.
   - ○ d. December.

8. On which day are carrot sticks on the menu?
   - ○ a. Monday
   - ○ b. Tuesday
   - ○ c. Wednesday
   - ○ d. Thursday

9. Which milk offered by the cafeteria is lowest in calories?
   - ○ a. lowfat chocolate
   - ○ b. skim
   - ○ c. 2%
   - ○ d. whole

10. The meal with the highest number of calories is served on
    - ○ a. Tuesday.
    - ○ b. Wednesday.
    - ○ c. Thursday.
    - ○ d. Friday.

Science Experiment

Purpose: Determine the most efficient light bulb. The bulb that gives off the least heat energy is the most efficient.

Hypothesis: The type of light bulb used will affect energy efficiency.

Materials Needed:
      Incandescent bulb, 60 watt
      *Fluorescent bulb, equal to 60 watt
      LED bulb, equal to 60 watts
      Thermometer
      Lamp

Procedure:
Step 1: Screw the incandescent light bulb into the lamp socket.
Step 2: Turn on the lamp.
Step 3: For one minute, hold the thermometer 15 cm above the bulb. Record the temperature (°C) in the data table below.
Step 4: Turn the lamp off, and let the bulb cool. Repeat steps 2 and 3 two more times.
Step 5: Repeat steps 1 through 4 with the fluorescent and LED bulbs.

Results: Record the temperatures (°C) in the data table below. For each type of bulb, calculate the average for the three trials. Record the answer.

Most Efficient Light Bulb				
Type of Bulb	**Trial #1**	**Trial #2**	**Trial #3**	**Average Temperature (°C)**
Incandescent bulb				
Fluorescent bulb				
LED bulb				

Analysis: Study the results of your experiment. Create a graph that will compare the average temperature for the three types of bulbs.

Conclusion: Write a summary of the experiment (what actually happened). It should include a brief description of the procedure and whether or not the hypothesis was supported by the data collected.

*Caution: Fluorescent bulbs contain a trace amount of mercury. Adult supervision is recommended for this experiment.

Science Experiment: Assessment

Name: _____   **Date:** _____

Directions: Fill in the bubble next to the correct answer for each multiple-choice question.

1. How many bulbs are needed for the experiment?
   - ○ a. 1
   - ○ b. 3
   - ○ c. 5
   - ○ d. 7

2. Which step comes immediately after placing a bulb in the lamp?
   - ○ a. record the temperature
   - ○ b. let the bulb cool
   - ○ c. turn on the lamp
   - ○ d. hold a thermometer above the bulb

3. How many minutes do you hold the thermometer above the blub?
   - ○ a. 1
   - ○ b. 3
   - ○ c. 4
   - ○ d. 15

4. Why is adult supervision recommended for this experiment?
   - ○ a. An electrical lamp is needed.
   - ○ b. A fluorescent bulb contains mercury.
   - ○ c. The adult holds the thermometer.
   - ○ d. The adult records the temperatures.

5. Which scale do you use to record the temperature of the bulb?
   - ○ a. Celsius
   - ○ b. Centrifuge
   - ○ c. Fahrenheit
   - ○ d. Kelvin

6. The purpose of the experiment is to find out
   - ○ a. which bulb produces the least heat energy.
   - ○ b. which is the longest lasting light bulb.
   - ○ c. which bulb produces the most light.
   - ○ d. which bulb cools the fastest.

7. In which step of the scientific method are you asked to create a graph?
   - ○ a. Purpose
   - ○ b. Hypothesis
   - ○ c. Analysis
   - ○ d. Conclusion

8. Which measurement is to be recorded on the table?
   - ○ a. length
   - ○ b. temperature
   - ○ c. time
   - ○ d. weight

9. How many times do you test each blub?
   - ○ a. 1
   - ○ b. 2
   - ○ c. 3
   - ○ d. 4

10. In which step of the scientific method are you asked to write a summary?
    - ○ a. Purpose
    - ○ b. Hypothesis
    - ○ c. Analysis
    - ○ d. Conclusion

Student Handbook

Lincoln Middle School
Student Handbook

page 22

CELL PHONES:
Students are allowed to bring cell phones to school as long as they follow the rules outlined in this policy. Cell phones must be turned off during the school day. The exceptions to this rule are before the first school bell rings, after the school dismissal bell, or with the direct supervision of a faculty or staff member. If a student violates this policy, the phone will be taken away. A parent or guardian will be responsible for picking up the phone from the principal. Students who are required to serve time in the in-school suspension (ISS) room **must surrender** their cell phones to the room monitor upon entering the ISS room.

CROSSWALK SAFETY:
There are four school crosswalks that will aid students in crossing the street safely. Students should cross streets only at one of the four designated crossings. When crossing the street, be alert and watchful at all times. Do not assume that drivers of vehicles are paying attention and/or will obey traffic signs. Before entering the crosswalk, make sure all cars have come to a complete stop. Do not run or loiter in the crosswalk, but proceed across in a cautious and courteous manner. Students who choose not to follow these rules will be required to meet with the school's safety officer and/or principal.

DANCES:
The Lincoln Middle School Student Council will sponsor two school dances each year. Only students in grades seven and eight who are currently enrolled at Lincoln Middle School are eligible to attend. The following will cause a student to be ineligible to attend:
- more than one day in ISS,
- more than 4 one-hour stays in ISS,
- one out-of-school suspension (OSS), or
- failure to meet Lincoln's attendance policy requirements.

Note: Once students leave the building, they will not be allowed to reenter the dance.

Student Handbook: Assessment

Name: _____ **Date:** _____

Directions: Fill in the bubble next to the correct answer for each multiple-choice question.

1. What is the consequence for leaving the building during a school dance?
   - ○ a. one day in ISS
   - ○ b. out-of-school suspension
   - ○ c. not allowed to attend the next school dance
   - ○ d. not allowed to reenter the dance

2. In the Student Handbook document, the cell phone policy is on page
   - ○ a. 20.
   - ○ b. 22.
   - ○ c. 24.
   - ○ d. 26.

3. Students are **not** allowed to use their cell phones
   - ○ a. before the first school bell.
   - ○ b. after the school dismissal bell.
   - ○ c. at lunch time.
   - ○ d. with supervision of a faculty member.

4. OSS is an abbreviation for
   - ○ a. one day of in-school suspension.
   - ○ b. one hour of in-school suspension.
   - ○ c. one day of out-of-school suspension.
   - ○ d. out-of-school suspension.

5. What is the maximum number of school dances the student council is allowed to sponsor each year?
   - ○ a. 1
   - ○ b. 2
   - ○ c. 3
   - ○ d. 4

6. According to the handbook, students may bring cell phones to school if
   - ○ a. they follow cell phone policy.
   - ○ b. their parents give permission.
   - ○ c. they follow cell phone safety rules.
   - ○ d. they participate in sports.

7. Which crosswalk safety rule is **not** included in the student handbook?
   - ○ a. be alert and watchful
   - ○ b. make sure cars have come to a complete stop
   - ○ c. proceed across in a cautious manner
   - ○ d. wait for the signal to cross

8. According to the student handbook, one OSS will cause a student to be ineligible to
   - ○ a. attend a school dance.
   - ○ b. enter the annual talent contest.
   - ○ c. join math club.
   - ○ d. participate in school sports.

9. Students who do not obey crosswalk rules will be required to
   - ○ a. attend pedestrian safety class.
   - ○ b. meet with the principal.
   - ○ c. receive one day of OSS.
   - ○ d. serve one day in ISS.

10. What is the consequence for violating the cell phone policy?
    - ○ a. lunch ISS
    - ○ b. in-school suspension
    - ○ c. out-of-school suspension
    - ○ d. phone taken away

Website Page

Home | Start Over | Help | About Us

Book reviews for kids by kids

New Books for October

Footsteps in the Night by Cory Flowers
After everyone has gone to bed, have you ever heard bumps in the night, floorboards creaking, or sounds of footsteps? This happened to George on the first night in his new home. The next day, George found out a murder had taken place in the house twenty years before. The crime had never been solved. Were the sounds that George heard linked to the crime? Could it be the ghost of the murder victim? If you like a good mystery, read *Footsteps in the Night* by Cory Flowers. 230 pages
                                        Johnny McBaine, 7th grade
                                        Cameron Middle School

Haunting of Collie Holler by Paul Quinton
A light has been seen late at night in the Collie Holler Cemetery. The police have investigated, but they can't find an explanation for the light. Danielle, Kate, and Dallas, three friends who live in Collie Holler, decide to conduct their own investigation. They stake out the cemetery and wait for the light. Around midnight, the light mysteriously appears in the back of the eerie graveyard. Are the friends brave enough to find out where the light is coming from? Read this scary book, but make sure you leave the lights on! 175 pages
                                        April Flood, 6th grade
                                        Madison Middle School

Paul Revere Takes a Ride by Tiffany Smith
You've probably heard about Paul Revere's famous ride to Concord and Lexington to warn the colonists about the approach of British soldiers. Did you know Revere was captured by British soldiers before he reached Concord? This is only one of the many interesting facts revealed in the book, *Paul Revere Takes a Ride.* The book is nonfiction, but it is written in an easy-to-understand way. This book would be a good choice for kids who want to learn more about Paul Revere or just need information for a research paper. 126 pages
                                        Daryl Ketchum, 8th grade
                                        Stull Academy

Bump in the Night and Other Silly Stories by Flora Fortune
This book is full of short stories that you will love to read. My favorite story was "I Saw a Skeleton Walking Down Willow Road." It was really funny. If you read this book, I know the stories will make you laugh out loud. 88 pages
                                        Molly Williams, 5th grade
                                        East Intermediate School

Home | About Us | Privacy Policy | How to Search Tips | Help

Website Page: Assessment

Name: _____   **Date:** _____

Directions: Fill in the bubble next to the correct answer for each multiple-choice question.

1. Which book is nonfiction?
   - ○ a. *Foolsteps in the Night*
   - ○ b. *Haunting of Collie Holler*
   - ○ c. *Paul Revere Takes a Ride*
   - ○ d. *Bump in the Night and Other Silly Stories*

2. Which is **not** the title of a link?
   - ○ a. Home
   - ○ b. Privacy Policy
   - ○ c. How to Search Tips
   - ○ d. Book Reviews for Kids by Kids

3. Which link should you click on to learn about the creator of the website?
   - ○ a. About Us
   - ○ b. Start Over
   - ○ c. Home
   - ○ d. Help

4. Which book was written by Paul Quinton?
   - ○ a. *Foolsteps in the Night*
   - ○ b. *Haunting of Collie Holler*
   - ○ c. *Paul Revere Takes a Ride*
   - ○ d. *Bump in the Night and Other Silly Stories*

5. Which student reviewer attends Madison Middle School?
   - ○ a. April Flood
   - ○ b. Cory Flowers
   - ○ c. Paul Quinton
   - ○ d. Molly Williams

6. Who is not a character in the book *Haunting of Collie Holler*?
   - ○ a. Danielle
   - ○ b. Kate
   - ○ c. Dallas
   - ○ d. April

7. The book reviews are for the month of
   - ○ a. February.
   - ○ b. April.
   - ○ c. July.
   - ○ d. October.

8. The book reviews were written by
   - ○ a. teachers.
   - ○ b. principals.
   - ○ c. students.
   - ○ d. librarians.

9. Which book reviewer is in the eighth grade?
   - ○ a. Johnny McBaine
   - ○ b. Paul Quinton
   - ○ c. April Flood
   - ○ d. Daryl Ketchum

10. Which book has the most pages?
   - ○ a. *Footsteps in the Night*
   - ○ b. *Haunting of Collie Holler*
   - ○ c. *Paul Revere Takes a Ride*
   - ○ d. *Bump in the Night and Other Silly Stories*

Bulletin Board Ideas

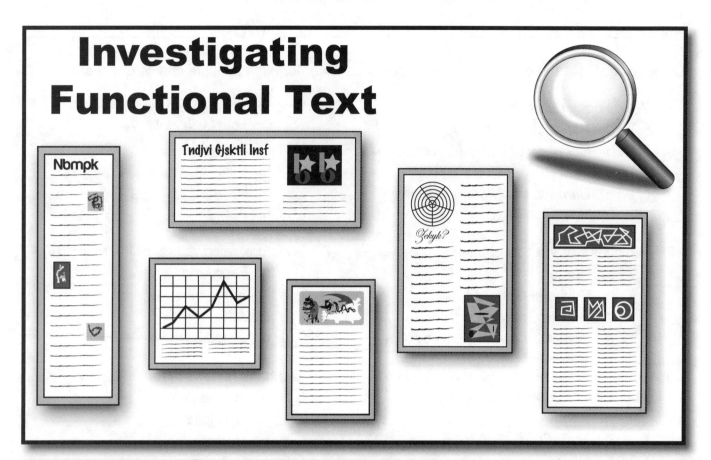

Bulletin Board Patterns

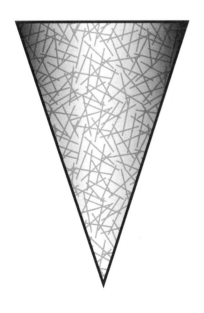

Text Mapping

Text mapping is a teaching tool. This method utilizes a graphic organizer. It starts with creating a scroll of pages from an old textbook. Students work in teams highlighting and labeling different text features they find on their section of the scroll.

Directions

Step 1: Take apart an old social studies or science textbook.

Step 2: Divide students into small groups.

Step 3: Give each group a section of the book.

Step 4: Instruct each group to tape or glue the pages together to make a horizontal scroll.

Step 5: Display the scroll on a wall, the floor, or a long table.

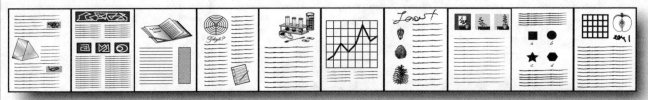

Step 6: Using a colored marker for each text feature, students highlight and label the features located on their section of the scroll.

Step 7: Groups share their completed project with the class.

Text Feature Wall

Text features are often overlooked by students. An interactive **text feature wall** is an effective way to help students identify and understand the usage of text features.

Directions

Step 1: With the class, review nonfiction text features.

Step 2: Using roll paper, cover a large area of the wall.

Step 3: Using a marker, divide the paper into box-like sections. Label each box with the name of a text feature.

Step 4: Have students cut out examples of text features from magazines and newspaper. Students glue the items inside the correct box on the wall chart.

Step 5: Use the wall chart as a reference when students are writing nonfiction text.

Functional Text Collection Notebook

Name: _____ **Date:** _____

Directions: Create a collection notebook in order to help you identify the different types of functional text. You will be asked to analyze the documents in your collection.

1. Collect samples of informational text documents, such as a menu, game rules, or a brochure. Some of the documents can be ones that you have created yourself, such as a letter, an email, or a recipe.

2. Complete the form below for each item in your collection notebook and attach it to the document.

3. Organize the documents into a collection. Create a table of contents that shows the order of your documents.

4. The collection should be submitted in an $8\frac{1}{2}$ X 11 binder, a pocket folder, or a notebook.

- -

Title: _____

Type of functional text document: _____

What is the author's purpose for creating the document? _____

_____

Objectively summarize the information in the document. _____

_____

_____

Text Features: Examine the functional text document and highlight any text features. On the form below, place a check mark next to each feature you find.

☐	Titles or Headings	☐	Labels/Captions
☐	Subtitles or Subheadings	☐	Graphs/Charts
☐	Print (Bold, Color, or Italic)	☐	Maps
☐	Glossary	☐	Tables
☐	Index	☐	Time Lines
☐	Table of Contents	☐	Diagrams
☐	Photographs	☐	Sidebars/Information Boxes
☐	Other _____		

Answer Keys

Practice Activities
Classified Advertisements (p. 4)
1. 142 Hayward Street   **2.** Lab   **3.** Pets/Pet Supplies
4. $5.00; The rate is 25 cents per word.
5. must be submitted by

Email (p. 6) 1. Shawn Howard   **2.** Math homework; I have attached my math homework.   **3.** Arial   **4.** inform teacher of absence and send homework   **5.** correct

Family Calendar (p. 8) 1. Susan   **2.** honor choir
3. family game night   **4.** It is the only Saturday night without any scheduled activities; Calendar for that date is blank.   **5.** January 30

Food Nutrition Label (p. 10) 1. Yum Yum; Yum Yum has 12g of sugar and Multi Grain has 6g.   **2.** Multi Grain
3. whole grain corn   **4.** 32g   **5.** Answers will vary, but may include: whole grain wheat, sugar, whole grain oats, salt, whole grain barley, fructose, corn syrup

Internet Search Screen (p. 12) 1. How to Search Tips
2. horses   **3.** www.horseshorseshorses.net
4. Breeds of Horses; horses that can be found on six different continents   **5.** breeding programs

Recipe (p. 14) 1. 4   **2.** Too much air left inside may force the bag to open during shaking.   **3.** 5–8 min.
4. 1 cup; doubled the 1/2 cup milk   **5.** reduces

Restaurant Menu (p. 16) 1. homestyle minestrone soup; $3.95   **2.** 18″   **3.** From Our Ovens to Your Table
4. 4 to 5   **5.** $14.50

Safety Rules (p. 18) 1. lifeguard; Swimming is allowed only when a lifeguard is on duty.   **2.** 10   **3.** 10:30 a.m. to 11 p.m.   **4.** concession stand area   **5.** food and beverages

Sales Flyer (p. 20) 1. XXL   **2.** $36.00   **3.** October 15
4. 2; white/blue and gray/blue   **5.** Come Soar With Us
Apply:

Text Message (p. 21) 1. Are you going to the game tonight? I need a ride. Can you pick me up? Let me know. Thanks.   **2.** Answers will vary.

Learning Stations Activity
Station One: Vocabulary (p. 24) Answers will vary.
Station Two: Real-Life Scenarios (p. 25)
Scenario One: No; "Attempts by the consumer to have

this product repaired will void this warranty," or "What is not covered by the warranty? unauthorized attempts to repair"
Scenario Two: No; "What is not covered by the warranty? products that were sold 'AS IS'"
Station Three: Returns (p. 26)
1. Horizons Manufacturing Company, Attn: Returns Department, 310 N. Randolph Street, Anytown, USA 78925
2. December 23, 2013   **3.** Burgess Electronics
4. consumer   **5.** remote control and owner's manual
6. HR-7500   **7.** Mary Cameron
Station Four: Details, Details, Details (p. 27)
1. one year   **2.** Horizons   **3.** television
4. 1-555-123-6789   **5.** retailer   **6.** Answers will vary.
7. repaired or exchanged for a similar product
8. refund or product exchange   **9.** state laws
10. Answers will vary.

Assessment Prep
Assembly Instructions (p. 29)
1. c **2.** a **3.** c **4.** b **5.** d **6.** b **7.** b **8.** c **9.** c **10.** a

Brochure (p.31)
1. c **2.** a **3.** c **4.** d **5.** a **6.** c **7.** d **8.** c **9.** d **10.** b

Bus Schedule (p. 33)
1. c **2.** a **3.** c **4.** a **5.** d **6.** d **7.** c **8.** b **9.** c **10.** b

Calendar of Events (p. 35)
1. b **2.** a **3.** b **4.** d **5.** c **6.** d **7.** b **8.** a **9.** b **10.** b

Class Schedule (p. 37)
1. b **2.** c **3.** c **4.** a **5.** c **6.** d **7.** b **8.** d **9.** d **10.** a

Game Rules (p. 39)
1. b **2.** a **3.** b **4.** c **5.** a **6.** a **7.** a **8.** d **9.** b **10.** d

Mall Directory (p. 41)
1. d **2.** b **3.** d **4.** c **5.** b **6.** b **7.** a **8.** a **9.** c **10.** b

Movie Guide (p. 43)
1. c **2.** d **3.** b **4.** c **5.** a **6.** a **7.** b **8.** c **9.** c **10.** a

Permission Letter (p. 45)
1. b **2.** a **3.** b **4.** b **5.** c **6.** b **7.** d **8.** c **9.** b **10.** a

Poster (p. 47)
1. d **2.** a **3.** c **4.** d **5.** a **6.** b **7.** c **8.** b **9.** b **10.** a

School Lunch Menu (p. 49)
1. b **2.** a **3.** d **4.** a **5.** c **6.** d **7.** a **8.** d **9.** b **10.** d

Science Experiment (p. 51)
1. b **2.** c **3.** a **4.** b **5.** a **6.** a **7.** c **8.** b **9.** c **10.** d

Student Handbook (p. 53)
1. d **2.** b **3.** c **4.** d **5.** b **6.** a **7.** d **8.** a **9.** b **10.** d

Website Page (p. 55)
1. c **2.** d **3.** a **4.** b **5.** a **6.** d **7.** d **8.** c **9.** d **10.** a